This book belongs to

_____

Children's Way of the Cross

by Anne Joan Flanagan, FSP
illustrated by Dick Smolinski

Pauline
BOOKS & MEDIA
Boston

Nihil Obstat:
Reverend Thomas W. Buckley, STD, SSL

Imprimatur:
+Bernard Cardinal Law
September 9, 1992

Published by Pauline Books & Media, 50 Saint Paul's
Avenue, Boston, MA 02130-3491. www.pauline.org.

Printed in U.S.A.

Pauline Books & Media is the publishing house of the
Daughters of St. Paul, an international congregation of
women religious serving the Church with the communica-
tions media.

7 8 9 10 11 12 13   12 11 10 09 08 07 06

Introduction

Scripture scholars tell us that the accounts of the suffering, death and resurrection of Jesus are the oldest kernels of the written Gospels. For the early preachers of the Good News, the Passion was the heart of their message.

The Passion of Jesus continued to speak to the hearts of believers. Throughout history, the followers of Jesus have looked for new ways to enter into that mystery, and so to find the meaning hidden in their own sufferings. The "Way of the Cross" is one way of meditating on Jesus' passage through death to life.

The prayers and meditations offered in this booklet have been specially written to help children enter into the mystery of Christ's suffering, death and resurrection. Each station opens with a suggestion of prayer for persons in today's world who are immersed in the sufferings of Christ. Adapting St. Ignatius' approach to meditation, the format allows children to use their gift of imagination to re-create the scene suggested in each station, and to place themselves there. A Scripture reading suggests the way this station applies to everyday life. A Scriptural response follows.

How to Use This Booklet

The prayers, readings and reflections in this booklet are arranged in a way that allows several children to assist the leader. This child-participation is important if the children are to feel that this is their prayer. Since Scripture texts are quoted from the *International Children's Bible*, young readers will find them easy to pronounce and to understand.

The format of each station allows for two or three readers to assist the leader or catechist. (Parts are assigned only to "reader 1" and "reader 2".) An interval of silence should follow the "Imagine" reading, after which the leader can cue reader 1 for the next section of the station.

Too-frequent posture changes can be distracting. The format allows for standing through the opening of each station, and sitting or kneeling for the central parts ("Imagine" and "Listen"). Participants can then stand to "Respond," and remain standing for the opening of the next station. (It would be well if the leader announced these postures.)

Opening Prayer

All:

Dear Jesus, who died to save me, I am here to remember your great love for me. I am sorry for the times I have not returned your love. May these Stations of the Cross open my heart more and more to your gifts of love!

✝ First Station

Leader:
First Station: Jesus Is Condemned to Death
Reader 1:
Pray for people who cause others to suffer.

Leader: We adore you, Christ; we praise you.

All: By your cross, you saved the world.

IMAGINE

Reader 2:

Jesus' enemies captured him. They made fun of him all night. They really wanted to kill him, but someone else had to do it. So they brought Jesus to Pilate. You are there. You can see that Pilate is going to do what the crowd says. What do you want to say to Jesus as Pilate condemns him to death?

LISTEN

Reader 1:

Christ suffered for you. He gave you an example to follow. So you should do as he did.

"He did no sin.
He never lied."

People insulted Christ, but he did not insult them in return. Christ suffered, but he did not threaten. He let God take care of him. *(1 Peter 2:21-23)*

RESPOND

All:

You saved me when the people attacked me.
    You made me the leader of nations.
(Psalm 18:43)

† Second Station

Leader:
Second Station: Jesus Takes Up His Cross
Reader 1:
Pray for people who are in pain.

Leader: We adore you, Christ; we praise you.

All: By your cross, you saved the world.

IMAGINE

Reader 2:

A big wooden cross gets laid across Jesus' shoulders. He will have to carry it for blocks and blocks. Let Jesus know that you are going to follow him the whole way.

LISTEN

Reader 1:

Christ carried our sins in his body on the cross. He did this so that we would stop living for sin and start living for what is right. And we are healed because of his wounds. *(1 Peter 2:24)*

RESPOND

All:

I praise the Lord because he guides me.
  Even at night, I feel his leading.
(Psalm 16:7)

✝ Third Station

Leader:
Third Station: Jesus Falls the First Time
Reader 1:
Pray for the victims of violence.

Leader: We adore you, Christ; we praise you.

All: By your cross, you saved the world.

IMAGINE
Reader 2:

The crowded streets smell like dust and garbage. Jesus stumbles along with his heavy cross. Then he falls into the dirty street and the cross comes crashing down on him. He looks at you to help him up.

LISTEN
Reader 1:

If you are punished for doing wrong, there is no reason to praise you for bearing punishment. But if you suffer for doing good, and you are patient, then that pleases God. *(1 Peter 2:20)*

RESPOND
All:

Lord, answer me quickly.
I am getting weak.
(Psalm 143:7)

✠ Fourth Station

Leader:
Fourth Station: Jesus Meets His Mother
Reader 1:
Pray for people who live alone.

Leader: We adore you, Christ; we praise you.

All: By your cross, you saved the world.

IMAGINE

Reader 2:

Mary is following as close as she can.
Run to catch up with her. Take her hand. It
means a lot to her that you love Jesus, too.

LISTEN

Reader 1:

Simeon...said to Mary,"[Your son] will be
a sign from God that many people will not
accept.... And the things that will happen will
make your heart sad, too." *(Luke 2:34-35)*

RESPOND

All:

Lord,
"I have seen your Salvation with my own
    eyes.
    You have prepared him before all people.
    He is a light."
(Luke 2:30-32)

✝ Fifth Station

Leader:
Fifth Station: Simon of Cyrene Helps Jesus
Reader 1:
Pray for people who are treated unfairly.

Leader: We adore you, Christ; we praise you.

All: By your cross, you saved the world.

IMAGINE

Reader 2:

Jesus can hardly walk. So the soldiers pull a man from the crowd. "Carry that cross," they tell him. The man, Simon, doesn't want to get involved. Is there anything you can tell Simon?

LISTEN

Reader 1:

Do not forget those who are in prison. Remember them as if you were in prison with them. Remember those who are suffering as if you were suffering with them. *(Hebrews 13:3)*

RESPOND

All:

The Lord God helps me.

So I will not be ashamed.
(Isaiah 50:7)

✝ Sixth Station

Leader:
Sixth Station: Veronica Wipes Jesus' Face
Reader 1:
Pray for people who dedicate their time to
helping others.

Leader: We adore you, Christ; we praise you.

All: By your cross, you saved the world.

IMAGINE

Reader 2:

The dry sand kicked up from the street is getting in your eyes and nose. You can even taste the dirt. But you keep going. Up ahead, a lady pushes past the soldiers and wipes Jesus' face with a cool, wet towel. Aren't you glad that someone was so brave and kind?

LISTEN

Reader 1:

"I was hungry, and you gave me food. I was thirsty, and you gave me something to drink. I was alone and away from home and you invited me into your house. I was without clothes, and you gave me something to wear. I was sick, and you cared for me. I was in prison, and you visited me.... Anything you did for any of my people here, you also did for me." *(Matthew 25:35-40)*

RESPOND

All:

...give thanks to the Lord for his love...
He satisfies the thirsty.

He fills up the hungry.
(Psalm 107:8-9)

✝ Seventh Station

Leader:
Seventh Station: Jesus Falls the Second Time
Reader 1:
Pray for people who are discouraged.

Leader: We adore you, Christ; we praise you.

All: By your cross, you saved the world.

IMAGINE
Reader 2:

As the sad parade moves through the city, Jesus falls again. This time, you are too far away to help. Look through the crowd. Is there anyone around who might give Jesus a hand?

LISTEN
Reader 1:

If God is with us, then no one can defeat us. God let even his own Son suffer for us. God gave his Son for us all. So with Jesus, God will surely give us all things. Who can accuse the people that God has chosen? No one! *(Romans 8:31-33)*

RESPOND
All:

The Lord is my light and the one who saves me.
   I fear no one.
(Psalm 27:1)

✝ Eighth Station

Leader:
Eighth Station: Jesus Meets the Good Women
Reader 1:
Pray for families that are having problems.

Leader: We adore you, Christ; we praise you.

All: By your cross, you saved the world.

IMAGINE
Reader 2:

Is that the sound of crying? You turn to see a group of women coming near Jesus. Some men in the crowd start to make fun of the women, but Jesus gives them his attention.

LISTEN
Reader 1:

God chose you to be his people. I tell you now to live the way God's people should live. Always be humble and gentle. Be patient and accept each other with love. *(Ephesians 4:1-2)*

RESPOND
All:

...the Lord comforts his people.
  He will comfort those who suffer.
(Isaiah 49:13)

✝ Ninth Station

Leader:
Ninth Station: Jesus Falls the Third Time
Reader 1:
Pray for people who are addicted to alcohol, drugs, or harmful behavior.

Leader: We adore you, Christ; we praise you.

All: By your cross, you saved the world.

IMAGINE

Reader 2:

This is taking so long—and there's still a way to go. You're not sure if you can make it. Jesus seems to be going even more slowly than before. He might not make it either.

LISTEN

Reader 1:

There are still many things that Christ must still suffer through his body, the church. I am accepting my part of these things that must be suffered. I accept these sufferings in my body. I suffer for his body, the church. *(Colossians 1:24)*

RESPOND

All:

I love you, Lord. You are my strength.
The Lord is my rock, my protection, my
    Savior.
(Psalm 18:1-2)

✝ Tenth Station

Leader:
Tenth Station: Jesus' Clothes Are Torn Off
Reader 1:
Pray for those who live in poverty.

26

Leader: We adore you, Christ; we praise you.

All: By your cross, you saved the world.

IMAGINE
Reader 2:

By the time you get to the hill called "Calvary," your clothes are sticky with dirt and sweat. Then you realize that the soldiers are going to make Jesus get undressed, right in front of everybody. You look at Jesus' eyes. What are they saying to you?

LISTEN
Reader 1:

Can anything separate us from the love Christ has for us? Can troubles or problems or sufferings? If we have no food or clothes, if we are in danger, or even if death comes— can any of these things separate us from Christ's love? I am sure nothing can separate us from the love God has for us. (Romans 8:35,38)

RESPOND
All:

If an army surrounds me,
  I will not be afraid.
If war breaks out,
  I will trust the Lord.
(Psalm 27:3)

✝ Eleventh Station

Leader:
Eleventh Station: Jesus Is Nailed to the Cross
Reader 1:
Pray for people who are hurting inside.

Leader: We adore you, Christ; we praise you.

All: By your cross, you saved the world.

IMAGINE
Reader 2:

The cross is a mean and horrible way to die. How can people even do that to another person? How can they do it to Jesus? You see the huge nails and hide your face. Mary holds you tight.

LISTEN
Reader 1:

Those who belong to Christ Jesus have crucified their own sinful selves. They have given up their old selfish feelings and the evil things they wanted to do. We get our new life from the Spirit. So we should follow the Spirit. We must not be proud. We must not make trouble with each other. And we must not be jealous of each other. *(Galatians 5:24-26)*

RESPOND
All:

Those who do evil have been defeated.
They are overwhelmed; they cannot do evil any longer.
(Psalm 36:12)

✝ Twelfth Station

Leader:
Twelfth Station: Jesus Dies on the Cross
Reader 1:
Pray for people who are close to death.

Leader: We adore you, Christ; we praise you.

All: By your cross, you saved the world.

IMAGINE

Reader 2:

You can't believe how long you've been here on this rocky hill. You squint your eyes to look up at Jesus on his cross. He looks back at you, but he can't say more than a few prayers to his Father. He is breathing very slowly.

The sky gets dark all of a sudden. Then everything grows quiet.

LISTEN

Reader 1:

Christ Jesus...was equal with God.

But...he gave up his place with God and
  made himself nothing.

He...became like a servant...and was fully
  obedient to God...even when that caused
    his death—death on a cross.

So God raised Christ to the highest place.
  God made the name of Christ greater than
    every other name. *(Philippians 2:5-9)*

RESPOND

All:

The ropes of death bound me.
  The fear of death took hold of me.
  I was troubled and sad.
Then I called out the name of the Lord.
  I said, "Please, Lord, save me!"
(Psalm 116:3-4)

✝ Thirteenth Station

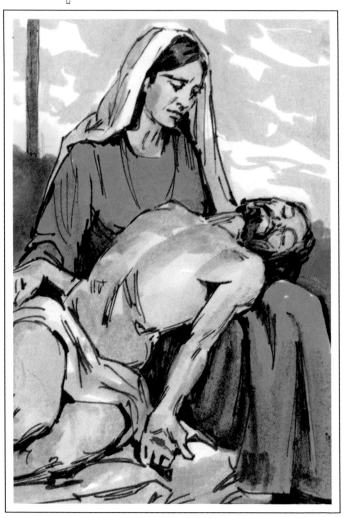

Leader:
Thirteenth Station: Jesus Is Taken from the Cross

Reader 1:
Pray for people who have died.

Leader: We adore you, Christ; we praise you.

All: By your cross, you saved the world.

IMAGINE
Reader 2:

Sometimes grown-ups seem uncomfortable having children around. Funerals are like that. As the men take Jesus' body off the cross, you want to get out of their way. Is there someone you can go to?

LISTEN
Reader 1:

All I want is to know Christ and the power of his rising from death. I want to share in Christ's sufferings and become like him in his death. If I have those things, then I have hope that I myself will be raised from death. *(Philippians 3:10-11)*

RESPOND
All:

I keep the Lord before me always....
So I rejoice, and I am glad.
   Even my body has hope.
This is because you will not leave me in the
   grave.
(Psalm 16:8-10)

✝ Fourteenth Station

Leader:
Fourteenth Station: Jesus Is Laid in the Tomb
Reader 1:
Pray for people who live in fear.

Leader: We adore you, Christ; we praise you.

All: By your cross, you saved the world.

IMAGINE
Reader 2:

Everything is quiet except for the shuffling of feet as people leave the cave. You take one look back inside before the others push that huge rock in front of the entrance. The body of Jesus, covered with cloth, has been buried. It's time to go.

LISTEN
Reader 1:

We have sufferings now. But the sufferings we have now are nothing compared to the great glory that will be given to us. Everything that God made is waiting with excitement for the time when God will show the world who his children are. *(Romans 8:18-19)*

RESPOND
All:

Because I have lived right, I will see your
   face.
   When I wake up, I will see your likeness
      and be satisfied.
(Psalm 17:15)

✝ Fifteenth Station

Leader:

Fifteenth Station: Jesus Rises from the Dead

Reader 1:

Pray for people who need to find God in their lives.

Leader: We adore you, Christ; we praise you.

All: By your cross, you saved the world.

IMAGINE

Reader 2:

Why are people shouting so early in the morning?

What are the women saying? Jesus has been "raised"? What does that mean?

LISTEN

Reader 1:

God raised the Lord Jesus from death. And we know that God will also raise us with Jesus. God will bring us together with you, and we will stand before him.
(2 Corinthians 4:14)

RESPOND

All:

The power of the Lord has won the victory.
  With his power the Lord has done mighty
      things.
(Psalm 118:16)

Closing Prayer

All:

Dear Jesus, we have walked this way of the cross together: you, me, my friends, and all the people of the world. Show me how to keep walking with you and your people. Help me to share your nearness with others. Amen.

BOOKS & MEDIA

The Daughters of St. Paul operate book and media centers at the following addresses. Visit, call or write the one nearest you today, or find us on the World Wide Web, www.pauline.org

CALIFORNIA
3908 Sepulveda Blvd, Culver City, CA 90230	310-397-8676
5945 Balboa Avenue, San Diego, CA 92111	858-565-9181

FLORIDA
145 S.W. 107th Avenue, Miami, FL 33174	305-559-6715

HAWAII
1143 Bishop Street, Honolulu, HI 96813	808-521-2731
Neighbor Islands call:	866-521-2731

ILLINOIS
172 North Michigan Avenue, Chicago, IL 60601	312-346-4228

LOUISIANA
4403 Veterans Memorial Blvd, Metairie, LA 70006	504-887-7631

MASSACHUSETTS
885 Providence Hwy, Dedham, MA 02026	781-326-5385

MISSOURI
9804 Watson Road, St. Louis, MO 63126	314-965-3512

NEW JERSEY
561 U.S. Route 1, Wick Plaza, Edison, NJ 08817	732-572-1200

NEW YORK
150 East 52nd Street, New York, NY 10022	212-754-1110

PENNSYLVANIA
9171-A Roosevelt Blvd, Philadelphia, PA 19114	215-676-9494

SOUTH CAROLINA
243 King Street, Charleston, SC 29401	843-577-0175

TENNESSEE
4811 Poplar Avenue, Memphis, TN 38117	901-761-2987

TEXAS
114 Main Plaza, San Antonio, TX 78205	210-224-8101

VIRGINIA
1025 King Street, Alexandria, VA 22314	703-549-3806

CANADA
3022 Dufferin Street, Toronto, ON M6B 3T5	416-781-9131

BOOKS & MEDIA

$3.95

ISBN 0-8198-6954-6